CROSSROADS OF THE OTHER

San Francisco 1973 - 1980

by
Ken Wainio

San Francisco
1993

Androgyne Books
930 Shields Street
San Francisco, CA 94132

Frontpiece photograph:
    Antonio Turok "San Andres De Larrainzar"
    Chiapas Mexico (1980) © Impreso en Mexico Por
    Litografica Turmex, S.A. de C.V.

Some of these poems first appeared *In Bastard Angel, Montana Gothic, Vanishing Cab, La Mamelle, Transfer, Beatitude, Nexus, 19 + 1 An Anthology of San Francisco Poets* and a chapbook *My Nakedness Creates You*, Sternum Press, 1977.

A limited edition of this book was done in stone by Bob Moore of Locust Press and Record Company, PO Box 14611, Portland, Oregon (1992).

ISBN 1-879594-18-8

CONTENTS

PREFACE

It is not at all apparent where the "volcanic summit" in one of Ken Wainio's poems, "Ventriloquist," may actually be located in the physical world. True, his poetic space manifests land, sea, moon and starry scapes, marked, sustained and transformed by constant reverie and practiced attention to, and interaction with, an evidently fertile dream life. Nevertheless, it so happens this oneiric space perfectly complements his native and childhood haunts in the environs of Redwood Valley, a relatively pristine inland region a hundred miles almost due north of San Francisco. This is Pomo Indian country through which the Russian River flows, alternately life-sustaining or turbulent from pelting rains. This river was once lined with numerous villages of Pomo-speaking tribelets whose other discontinuous territories were spread north and east of the river, including the once idyllic region surrounding Clear Lake, the largest wholly within California. Risen from a nearby plain, overlooking the lake, is solitary Mount Konocti, whose name means Female Mountain, to this day covered by the bodily remains of the Herculean, supernatural being of Pomo myth, Obsidian Man, whose hard glassy black & brown parts are encountered strewn everywhere at the base of this once volcanic mountain.

This present collection belongs to Wainio's first decade or so of living in San Francisco, where apparently viable contact was made with a few of us attempting an extension of poetic surrealism. The three-part prose poem, "Letters From Rimbaud," is also a touchstone carrying an anticipatory sign of "a new country" that may await those whose "footsteps are seeds." Such interior journeys foreshadowed Wainio's season in Egypt (1979), which inspired his first published book of prose *Letters From*

Al-Kemi, a high-spirited travelogue, studded with his peculiar sense of humor, which also delineates a plausible self-portrait and whose opening sentence corresponds to what is most singular in his poetry. "It is true I have always felt a strong attraction to Ancient Egypt, her people and art, as if I possessed an innate race memory of that vanished culture, or found personal evidence in my reveries for the transmigration of souls."

Of poets who wrote in the English language it seems significant to mention certain central theoretical ideas that anticipated the surrealist project for poetry. Shelley with enthusiastic approval cites Milton's principle that his muse "dictated" to him "the unpremeditated song." Poe held in the highest estimation those involuntary images, "fancies" he called them, which rise from within us in privileged moments "between wakefulness and sleep." The very title, *Crossroads of the Other*, suggests that the poet has found the way to mediate composition, to paraphrase Andre Breton, from "communicating vessels" of unconscious sources of inspiration and conscious activity. This fertilizing relation, of conscious and unconscious mental perception, is the sole structure that allows the liberation of eroticized energy as a basic force field to determine a living poetic text in contradistinction to the passionless and contrived elucubrations of false poets. Erotic presence turns into poetic evidence. For Wainio the erotic-marvelous arrives on dove's feet, branded with suffering, clear-obscure, even, yet flashing redolent sparks and finally erupts highly condensed in the superb poem "Driving Through Mexico," celebrating a double victory of the road's freedom with animating fires lighting up the green source of eternal recurrence. Apposite to the erotic-marvelous, objective humor also erupts, by turns fantastic and absurd, as in "Bourgeoisie," subverting by a healthy misanthropy the hidden demonology of misdirected global societies of fragmented victims ("the living dead") that survive their decadence by ever more violent means -- ecocide and nuclear threat -- and through isolation of whatever exists of a tiny minority of beings attempting reintegration and resurrection of real life a true poet announced not too long ago, "is absent."

Philip Lamantia

FOR BOB KAUFMAN

"I am writing only for my shadow, which is now stretched across the wall in the light of the lamp. I must make myself known to him."

Sadegh Hedayat

WORLD NEWS BRIEF

THE SUN CAME UP SEVERAL HOURS EARLY THIS MORNING
WITNESSES REPORTED IT BEHAVING ODDLY AROUND 3 AM
IT WAS SAID TO BE LYING IN A PASTURE
ON TOP OF THE MOON
ONE WOMAN SAID THE STARS WERE ON THE GROUND
AND THE WHOLE HORIZON
LOOKED LIKE IT WAS BEING EXPLORED
WITH GIANT SEARCHLIGHTS

THREE DOGS CAUGHT FIRE ON A RANCHER'S PATIO
BUT WHEN INTERVIEWED
HE SAID THEIR BONES HAD BEEN PICKED CLEAN
BY THE LIGHT
AND HE HAD NO KNOWLEDGE
OF THEIR PRESENT WHEREABOUTS

POLICE SAY THE SUN WAS SOBER
WHEN TAKEN INTO CUSTODY THIS MORNING
AND BOOKED ON CHARGES OF DISTURBING THE PEACE
IT IS PRESENTLY BEING HELD PENDING TRIAL
BETWEEN OUR SOLAR SYSTEM
AND THE NEAREST STAR

FARMERS OFFERED TO BUY THE ROPES
HANGING FROM THE EMPTY HOLE IN THE SKY
BUT AUTHORITIES SAY THEY WILL BE
HANDED OVER TO THE CITY PLANNING COMMISSION
TO BE HOLLOWED OUT AND USED FOR SNAKEHOLES
IN THE LOCAL ZOO

THE SHADOW LEFT BY ITS ABSENCE
IS PRESENTLY BEING INVESTIGATED

NIGHT

Outside is the burden of night
stars sparkle between the reins
Inside my wife winks at me
and draws the blinds
I find a burning trail
in the closet where she has hidden
what saves me from tomorrow
Over the mantle is a shotgun
I train the barrel
on the operating table
She doesn't move
in a little while we turn the set off
and go to bed
Only the night could give you more
than simple light
Those of you who say you understand
the darkness that separates the stars

ANTHEM

Night. That much is for sure.

The wooden cloud of my desk floats in the lamp's orange eye. I am interpreting the news for a foreign paper which has its office not far from here in a skyscraping crypt: Several floors devoted entirely to the gathering of information which is already outdated by the time it finds its way into print.

I try not to feel out of place, but my heartbeat is somewhere around the moon.

I take note of the room.

The air is dusty, layered with smoke from my cigarette. My breathing is normal. The carpet flat on its belly. Walls bulging with books.

Everything normal.

Yet my heartbeat is somewhere beyond the moon and its shadow is leaving my skull.

The houses are clustered outside my window, the wind blowing creepers against the glass. In the distance, bloody sirens and burping foghorns.

I write the headlines of sleep, action, and order.
I open my eyes in the tomb. I collect the taxes of earth.
And I am patient.

But my heartbeat is beyond the moon.

I hear the click of a dog's nails on a neighbor's
porch. A soft breeze touches me on the face. The
shutter swings open revealing a star maze.

A woman is nodding beneath a white hat brim.
She is sitting in a tunnel ordering the traffic around. I
approach her cautiously and ask the way. She points in
the direction of my bones.

I turn the mirror to the wall and the nails click
down the steps. Spring is teasing the leaves and a
green vapor waves from the pond.

I am given identification papers by a woman from
the Interior. She leaves me standing at the border. The
authorities accuse me of being an impostor.

Summer and the grass is brown and dry.
Shadows nest under the trees. A buzzard hangs noon
high. The creek dissolves leaving a crust of hag's hair.

I am convicted of being an illegal alien and
sentenced to death. A gallows is constructed on the
dry hillside. I am given a number and told to wait my
turn. Only the sky is sympathetic, its blue hand resting
on my shoulder.

It motions to me with the birds.

Their wing beats thunder in the temples as I am taken to the gallows.

The trap door creaks beneath me. Sweat runs down the face of the hangman. He places the noose around my neck and reaches for the lever. The trap jerks open and the mirror spins around to another landscape.

I am in the Atlantic Museum looking at a study of the 20th century. The curator comes up and asks what I'm doing there. I tell him I'm looking for a portrait of myself. He smiles and calls the guard.

I am taken to the past and thrown in the drunk tank with the vampires of hungry memory. They drink the blood of another time and are possessed by the key to the door I imagine.

My heartbeat bailed out by stars.

TURN ON THE LIGHTS

The glass will not harm you
but sometimes it sweats in the groin of day
where it burns the dust on the feet of insects
and crawls through the flaming hairs of your fingers
pressed there to see if you can feel the invisible

And sometimes the steaming sex of night
drills its trumpet in your breast
to see if it can make you hear
the grinning notes of starlight
sweating music in your heart

So if silence comes on hands and knees
to fuck the holes you left in words
you will know the invisible has been made
and is standing in front of your empty house
waiting for you to come home and turn on
the lights

BUYING A CAR

It's like following a tarantula
through the wake of a desert
The heart seems to come closer to itself
till the mirage nears and disappears
The white face tugs at itself
It is not the moon
Or the eclipse
There is no shadow
The tunnel widens
till it is like nothing
you've ever seen before

On the other side
the water is pale with distance
Someone is standing on the shore
It is a very small child
holding a photograph in a frame
He is plotting his future
and wondering how long it will be
till his life begins

Out on the lake
something is moving
He raises his head to his eyes
and watches himself fade
till there is nothing left of it
and he is driving in a car
towards the flat horizon
His memory full of eyes
memorizing silence

COMING HOME FROM WORK

Standing first outside listening for my shoes
waiting to go in and listen to the abandoned

raga. Where have you been? Again the night
has eaten my coat and I have nothing in which

to hide. Only a furnished typewriter. So I
go in and sit down where there is a chair

placed just there for me. Put on the morning
raga and ignore the horde of waving shovels

in the street. You are inside and there is
nothing left to bury. Come in and write this

down. They have all gone to work and soon
their empty autos will be heating in the sun.

The lunch pails will be dead at noon. Drunken
testicles will overflow the bars. Nothing will

be left of the sun save the banks in the starving
fog. Nothing. I can hear your blood pulsing

in the moon. It is low tide and the mind is
ebbing away from the door. The shovels on their

way to work are miles away by this time. Sand
runs naked on the window sill and the wind is

trying to whistle a tune in the keyhole. Toccata
and Fugue in D minor I think. The cathedral

expands to Gothic proportions. Stained
glass rattlesnakes are welling in the dark arches

far above hunched over pews. A wedding is in
progress across from the funeral. They are

carrying the ashes from side to side. The organ
swells as the bride approaches the altar and

beckons to the groom. The alms bowl vomits blood
into the hands of a savage-faced priest. Why

couldn't my wedding have been this good? My heart
pumps vomit through the veins of my wallet. You

are not listening. The raga has turned your mind
to ash. The door is shut. By evening their

machines will be parked in the moonlight in front
of your house. The key turning in the lock and

the bellied-up lunch pails souring on the kitchen
sink.

MYTH

I am a more perfect drug
than has ever been invented

The babies in my celestial skull
scream for it

but do not understand why
I am really what they want

My words rattle in their baby rattles
and yet they do not understand

a thing I say. Bushes of laughter
well up in my criminal throat

and in my mythical gardens bloom curious
strains that cannot be deciphered

Lawmakers are frantic to break the code
but they only make the babies scream louder

Thus I ignite cockroach armies in their minds
and rock the crib of battlefields

in a small space between my fingers
A sign sometimes taken to mean very little

and sometimes to provide living quarters
for innumerable worlds

THE CROSSROADS

My grandfather always used to say
nothing is best. I couldn't have agreed more

until the day I found you
crowded in a shower in which the hot and cold
had been permanently reversed
Someone had taken your clothes

and you were afraid to come out because you thought
I would laugh. A carcass is saved by its own maggots

I told you snapping your buttocks with a towel
Pity you said rubbing the welt

We used to take long walks together
in the bashful afterglow of your vision
You would say. . .

wisdom is a snowflake in the desert
I said it is the drinking hole of ants
You looked at me with the eyes of a spider
and ran off in the trees
afraid of the dark. I laughed
and ran after you as I always did
armed with snapshots of holymen
and pornographic rainbows

We would always end at the crossroads
to contemplate the gallows beneath a sky
pelting us with cats and dogs

I would mount the steps and pretend to hang myself
You would pull your hair and weep until
I came down with a bit of shredded noose
for you to put in your scrapbook

And then there was the haunted house
What a time that was. I remember you standing

on the front steps holding a flashlight
for protection. Your courage melting like the smile
on the face of a distraught Avon Lady

I opened the door. . .

and you cast the beam around on the floor
Nothing there but an empty whisky bottle
and dusty space

We walked home stepping in puddles of melted fur
Such a shock it was for you

What did you expect to find there? My grandfather. . .
He died fifty years before you were born

He always said nothing is best. . .

I say you are right.

BOURGEOISIE

Build a motorcycle and drive it full speed through town with your girlfriend on the back. When you get out into the country stop at the first auto accident you see. Get off your bike and throw a lit cigarette in the gas tank. When the blaze subsides have your girlfriend help you scatter the pieces.

The second thing to do is learn how to speak. Get your girlfriend and yourself a couple of walkie-talkies. Send her to the mountains with an empty canteen and go yourself to the desert to look for water. Hitchhike back into town when you begin to die of thirst. Forget about your girlfriend. Throw the walkie-talkies away and forget any of it ever happened.

Now go to the drugstore. The thing you want to do here is learn how to listen. Stick a gun into the ribs of the person behind the counter and demand that he or she sing your favorite song. If they have forgotten the words make them take all the drugs in sight. Then push them out into the streets when they are good and stoned.

Now you are ready to write. When you know the crowd has gathered around the exploded motorcycle go retrieve your walkie-talkie, call your girlfriend in the mountains, and have her meet you at the accident with the glass of water you couldn't find in the desert. Have her throw it on the fire. This will delight the crowd. They will all get out of their cars. Face each other in two lines of disproportionate length, about four hundred years apart, and begin to dance. The auto accident victims will run down the space between them. This dance is called THE RUNNING OF THE GAUNTLET. All peoples, primitive and modem, practice it. The two lines of dancers are called UPPER and LOWER class. The long space in the middle down which the auto accident victims run is called the BOURGEOISIE.

The dancers in one of the classes, it's hard to say which, begin to hurl sharp objects, with incredible religious rapidity, at the most vulnerable parts of the dancers in the class opposite them. This disconcerts some of the dancers on both sides of THE GAUNTLET, causing them to split from the main body of the dance and gather into tribes. Soon they learn their own dance and only recall the old one when they drive into town for supplies.

Meanwhile the ancestral dance goes on. The auto accident victims continue to run THE GAUNTLET of the BOURGEOISIE. This is why the dance is sometimes called a GHOST DANCE. THE GAUNTLET is run only by THE SPIRITS OF THE DEAD, once belonging to the dancers of both classes whose bodies are now called THE LIVING DEAD.

Soon the fire will be out and the dancers will drive back into town to watch themselves on the news. Have your girlfriend help you bury the wreckage. Then build another motorcycle and drive far away. It will not pay for you to stick around, now that you understand how things are.

PIONEER TEN SENDS BACK 340 IMAGES OF JUPITER

The dream scale is weighing the closet again
and the Secretary of the Interior has parked

his garage in my head. I'm not sure when he's
coming out but any day now we should have

messages tape-recorded by the sun. Isn't this
a fine gyroscope he says handing me a camera.

It's beautiful I say holding it in my arms and
fluffing up its hair. Any day now the Egyptians

will walk out of the text books and hold up the
moon with a chocolate pistol. Any day now. . .

any day. . . any day. . . any day. . . .

ANARCHY

Should the walls crack open to reveal a battle
scar of flowers in a yellow field, then the hour has
come to bury the dead. I am not speaking of summer
aftermath or that green return of seasoned anarchy.
Nor does winter show its buried hand. "But when
does one write the poem?" ask the corners in rooms
at the meeting halls of spiders. "Does the dust of
illumination materialize in the wake of revolving
doors? Are the sequential spasms of time abolished?"
The sea has a plug that drains the cradle and the fish
are drunk in the saloons of shipwrecks. The wind
combs back its foggy hair and reveals a woman on the
edge of the surf where pillars rise, banners flap, and
hushed wings fall on the diamond sand.

GETTING RID OF THE EGO

It's like getting married in the rain. A coach will pull up at the edge of the dam when the flood starts and the bride throws her flowers at the drowned. If you don't believe this, go to a monastery for ten years and study the light through a keyhole. Without moving your eye from the door cut out a piece of sky and wait for somebody to come with a key.

The flood is well up by this time. The dead are getting married in rowboats and copulating on pieces of wreckage. If you still don't believe it, take out your keyhole and study the drowned. They are discussing the possibilities of islands and shaping tombstones into anchors. Their children hold their breath underwater and pray to the God of Rain. He is holding himself in a cloud making everybody worship the flood. He is quite fond of suffering and has never understood sociology. But the dead come with their pogo sticks and stare up at the seat of his pants.

If you still don't get this, go sit down in the nearest bar and study the runway of faces. If anyone comes up to you and demands your marriage certificate, take out your keyhole and blast them with a peak of stars. If they are still sitting there waiting for you to kill your ego, tell them the world is flat and has an edge like the table. Drop something transparent over the side and tell them it was the argument of Columbus on his way to the new world.

LETTERS FROM RIMBAUD

1.

The lantern with the black hooks swings above the doorway. It leads the light across the veranda down the steps of time. The street enters the coffee house. Its yellow windows grip my eyes. Cars float by on missing wings. Faces, unable to control expression, multiply and divide. There is an implosion of hair and flesh, drooling on passing strangers. Miles away I can hear a new country where the sky has not planted my eyes. Now footsteps are seeds.

2.

Vessels on the bay carry raving cargoes of starlight out to sea. Waves snap their fingers and bring webs of fog to the heart which has missed its target. The night discovers who it is stole the darts of the sky and flung them in the sea with the bones of stars and brains of lost anchors. The sails have proved the storm right for now the vessels are taking on the green shadows of the sea's undistilled childhood for the long journey home.

3.

The wind's jacket is on fire. It writes the moon's poems and sends flames by the mail, using its pockets for envelopes. Out on the pier the night coughs sailors on the waves who slap their watery thighs and laugh at nothing. The sky smirks back and a creek dribbles slowly from the lips of the moon. It puts out the fire the wind has started on the oily waves with the butt of a drunken captain. The pier watches calmly, glad the night's shining madman hasn't provoked the sun's destructive genius. Now the moon blinks in daylight and opens the water in its right eye.

OSIRIS

He has become Osiris. One cell at a time. Once eternally. He strides through the gloom of dawn at the mercy of his original toes. Little gangs of mist seethe between the gravestones where silence has become the sound of his tread. The Valley of Death holds no shadow and as he peers into the contents of each coffin, there is nothing inside save the mouldy offerings of various receptacles. The worms give off a multi-colored life glow, changing from endless shades of blue and metallic gray to pink, yellow, and turquoise luminosity. Yet their mystery has cast no spell over his vision which is colorless, white in the black night, a pinpoint of light glancing off his coffin, floating down the Nile.

Osiris moves off into the distance and watches life and death flash over the twilight lake of his senses. He counts each pair as their wings bathe the water with fluttering moonlight and then compares them to the number of stars frying into the darkening skillet of the night. From the universe in the empty socket of his skull, a beak protrudes. It is made up of matter and space is the master of its wings. He listens to it scrape against the lid of his coffin. The lid opens slowly and it is Isis adoring his remains. He discovers he is safe in the sudden bliss of her womb. His pain has been calmed and his despair has been soothed. The two of them walk hand in hand. He has become Osiris. One cell at a time. Once eternally.

HUNTING VOICES

I have been sad. I have been sad and corrupt as the soil. I have seen the white fox running in the trees. The lone hound flee its master's gaze. I have been cruel to the stars. I have milked the lake of flames. I fell from castle windows long before there was anything to lose. And yet I am alone in this stillness as if it caged some sorrow I cannot begin to understand. Now night casts down its unbrandished shield. Now creeks cross the fields like harps and are alone with their flowing voices.

In the town, a small boy stops by a puddle. His round face is a shadow pulled from sleep. He touches the sky touching nothing but himself. The wind has found its eyes in a mask of trees. It watches him gently through an applause of leaves.

He has buried his happiness by the lake where the dog comes with the hunter to drink from the gathered water. It is fed by a cemetery brook, a single flag on the door, its white hand hanging as if there were no game, and no sight.

The shade moves closer to the trees and the dog scratches on the door. The little boy removes his coat. It is red. Not unlike strawberries, it hangs on a twig like something pulled from the sea's blue mouth.

It is evening and singing. The waves break on shore. They need no forgiveness.

WHAT IS MOVING

What is moving
this circle of sunlight on the wall
what is moving
who has come with the bridle of journeys
spent wandering in the trash of sunlight
who has put this filing cabinet of heat
on the doorsill for the flies to bug
who is the one in trenchcoat silence
and why is he tearing shadows
from the backs of clouds
who has spread a tablecloth over the mirror
and why are reflections
dreaming of a feast
which moves deeper into the eye
what is moving
who has come to peer through the windows
where sand undresses the sea
what is moving
who has decided the color of the wind
is it gold
is it green
does it hang itself on nails
when frost comes to singe the windows
and the little children
race home for nothing
why are all the sails of memory flaming
when a shadow slides
across the forehead of a passing woman
and lights in the budhouse of the ear

what is moving
why why why
are the birds so charming
have they come from under the woman's dress
passing in the fog
has she left footprints
will the sea take them
when the sky has become clear
and nothing is moving
but a bright circle of birds
whose shadows cross the wall?

DRIVING THROUGH MEXICO

Wanting her
at the violent base
of the redcross hills
climbing up
the cliff face
in sacrificial
rainpools
swimming
to get to her
red and splitting open
at the jungle's edge
long before her presence
and absence are
one

Wanting her
along the wall of the red night clouds
wanting the fish in her belly
the rain in her mouth
the smoke of her joints
to fetch the darkness from my skull
hang its pinata of light
in a distant window
and rap on her trickling rays
the wind
between silent electric shocks
tossing the red fruit
of lovemaking in our eyes
driving the butterflies

over our terrified windshield
driving out everything
left to flee

Wanting her
at the jungle altar beside
the road we light the candles
and strip each other
delicately in the rain
Two crosses on bloody toes
we mount and ride
loping over suburbs
of breeding mosquitoes
the animals trailing us licking
the notes of our blood
from the fallen leaves
lapping from the green pools
at our feet the weird exotic
cocktails of our suffering thankful
there is someone to distill the mescal
of love gods in the pulqueria
of our dubbed-in voices

RAIN COWS

So night dooms understanding. Sex in a treadmill Love in a barnstorm. Death who sticks his finger in the whirling spokes. If you want to enter the cross of worlds, take the slap from my face. Put it in your bag and travel far from here. Let me see your hands. Let me dust your shadow. I love the nameless whine of all railroad yards.

In the cemetery, words tear like nylons. A lively caress hitching books of elixir wood. Our ears immaculate dice snap beneath giant feet. Don't tell me of footprints in the frozen wastes. Comets, grease spots on the turning hub, men jump from centuries to eons. I clap each one on their shattered backs. Welcome home! That ghost you saw back there was only the Milky Way. If there are no visible cows then forget the fences. There are no clouds but it feels like rain. . . .

VENTRILOQUIST

I am in love with my horse
It has always been this way
Ever since he danced on the lizard's back
I have been seasick without him
His hoofprints are boats
I follow across intangible earth
At the volcanic summit
my thoughts grinding in the clouds
are only his hoofprints upside down
I seek him in the rain
I follow him down the stormdrain
and reflect upon his shadow in the sea
I have no thoughts for others
because the looking glass has turned to water
and he is the first one I saw born
the night swimming was invented in the stars
I nurse him in dreams
when he has given birth to a nightmare
I seek out the intruder in his stall
and devour the afterbirth that has mothered him
I am his knowledge
though he is the pilgrim of all my concerns
and carries a whispering light
in every eye I meet along the dream road
A single candle in the night cannot discover him
and under the bed on which the rider sleeps
I hear him speak these words

WHATEVER SPEAKS DOESN'T SEEM TO

say a cloud in the sky. The sun's glare
in the mist along the cliff side, a
tiny seething of wet flames. What wanders
doesn't seem to cut the path in half. A
little water and what is left of salt
can be yours for a little more. The tongue
that softest of flames, how it does no
one insists, drifting in the coldest
currents, it spit red. The sea knows
its roar a sound hydrant, circumspect
a discussion of riot, but an airtight star
the ear plugs in, O nightlife that has
lost its secret rendezvous

MORNING

In the morning I
come down from the hills
I come down like a broken promise
from the hills
and no
even though it
is not really morning
but already far
into the flyspeck of
another afternoon
I come down to the magic
coming of words
that have no promise
other than themselves
I come down
because the dead stand
in the wings
and whisper the frog of pain
in my sticky coffee cup
toasting the possibility
of anything there is
to come down to
here on this white carpet
of pulverized noise
on this very blue sea
of fizzing light
when afternoon is the nook
of evening and the great
hope of catastrophe

is silent on the battlements
of how things should be
this way or that
when I come down in
the morning when you
come down in the
morning when I come down
from the beautiful
drug of sleep
to find you
alone

POSTMORTEM

The locations of poems, sites of transmission, are more interesting to me than what's in the coffins. "Letters From Rimbaud," for instance, arrived downstairs one evening in the old Malvinas Cafe, Union Street, San Francisco, 1974, an hour or so before Bob Kaufman started talking again, wildly, after a long silence, of "Solitudes Crowded With Loneliness." Or "Osiris," Bob's favorite corpse of mine, written twilight, Horse Mountain, Lake County, 1973, employed by "Smith Air" to hustle copter fuel around the backwoods, helping forestry crews put out snag fires, smoking local stuff and reading "The Egyptian Book of the Dead." Or "Pioneer Ten" which came in with the morning paper and the SLA, Prospect Street, 1974. Or more accurately, fresh out of bed, "Bourgeoisie," Grant Avenue, 1976, naked, shaking with hangover, hands like gloves worn by somebody else, taking dictation. Or "Ventriloquist," Stuttgart, Germany, 1979, in a friend's apartment, listening to music and pining over French woman left in Greece, St. George screwing his dragon on a jacket cover. Or "Driving Through Mexico," for the same woman, who was never in Mexico, where the poem insisted on taking place several years before during another trip, somebody else in the passenger seat, Jackson Street, 1980. All those afterlives still resonating, still keeping track of what anything is about, what sinks or swims or walks on wooden feet of fire, signatures of a journey up in smoke, remembered by nobody, save you, unknown reader. I kiss you like an old flame.

Ken Wainio
SF 5/91